DREW BREES, DEUCE MCALLISTER, CRAIG
HEYWARD, ERIC MARTIN, JOE HORN,
HENRY CHILDS, JAHRI EVANS, WILLIE
ROAF, JIM DOMBROWSKI, JAKE KUPP,
JERRY FONTENOT, WAYNE MARTIN, JOE
JOHNSON, LA'ROI GLOVER, JIM WILKS,
PAT SWILLING, SAM MILLS, VAUGHAN
JOHNSON, DAVE WAYMER, DAVE WHITSELL,
SAMMY KNIGHT, TOMMY MYERS, MORTEN
ANDERSEN, TOMMY BARNHARDT, DREW
BREES, DEUCE MCALLISTER, CRAIG
HEYWARD, ERIC MARTIN, JOE HORN,
HENRY CHILDS, JAHRI EVANS, WILLIE
ROAF, JIM DOMBROWSKI, JAKE KUPP

THE STORY OF THE NEW ORLEANS SAINTS

THE STORY OF THE NEW ORLEANS SAINTS

BY JIM WHITING

CREATIVE EDUCATION / CREATIVE PAPERBACKS

PUBLISHED BY CREATIVE EDUCATION AND CREATIVE PAPERBACKS
P.O. BOX 227, MANKATO, MINNESOTA 56002
CREATIVE EDUCATION AND CREATIVE PAPERBACKS ARE IMPRINTS OF THE
CREATIVE COMPANY
WWW.THECREATIVECOMPANY.US

DESIGN AND PRODUCTION BY BLUE DESIGN (WWW.BLUEDES.COM)
ART DIRECTION BY RITA MARSHALL
PRINTED IN CHINA

PHOTOGRAPHS BY AP IMAGES (ASSOCIATED PRESS), CORBIS (BETTMANN),
CREATIVE COMMONS WIKIMEDIA (HDELBOY.CLUB.FR), GETTY IMAGES
JONATHAN BACHMAN/STRINGER, BERNSTEIN ASSOCIATES, STEPHEN DUNN/
ALLSPORT, JOHN FITZHUGH/BILOXI SUN HERALD/MCT, CHRIS GRAYTHEN,
OTTO GREULE JR., JIM GUND, ANDY HAYT, WESLEY HITT, HARRY HOW/
ALLSPORT, JED JACOBSOHN, NICK LAHAM, NEIL LEIFER/SI, ED MAHAN/NFL
PHOTOS, RONALD MARTINEZ, AL MESSERSCHMIDT, DONALD MIRALLE, DON
JUAN MOORE, NFL PHOTOS, JOE ROBBINS, MANNY RUBIO/NFL PHOTOS, MARIO
TAMA, LOU WITT/NFL)

NAMES: WHITING, JIM, AUTHOR.
TITLE: THE STORY OF THE NEW ORLEANS SAINTS / JIM WHITING.
SERIES: NFL TODAY.
INCLUDES INDEX.
SUMMARY: THIS HIGH-INTEREST HISTORY OF THE NATIONAL FOOTBALL
LEAGUE'S NEW ORLEANS SAINTS HIGHLIGHTS MEMORABLE GAMES, SUMMARIZES
SEASONAL TRIUMPHS AND DEFEATS, AND FEATURES STANDOUT PLAYERS SUCH
AS DREW BREES.
IDENTIFIERS: LCCN 2018059136 / ISBN 978-1-64026-151-8 (HARDCOVER) / ISBN
978-1-62832-714-4 (PBK) / ISBN 978-1-64000-269-2 (EBOOK)
SUBJECTS: LCSH: NEW ORLEANS SAINTS (FOOTBALL TEAM)—HISTORY—
JUVENILE LITERATURE. / NEW ORLEANS SAINTS (FOOTBALL TEAM)—HISTORY.
CLASSIFICATION: LCC GV956.N366 W45 2019 / 796.332/640976335—DC23

FIRST EDITION HC 9 8 7 6 5 4 3 2 1
FIRST EDITION PBK 9 8 7 6 5 4 3 2 1

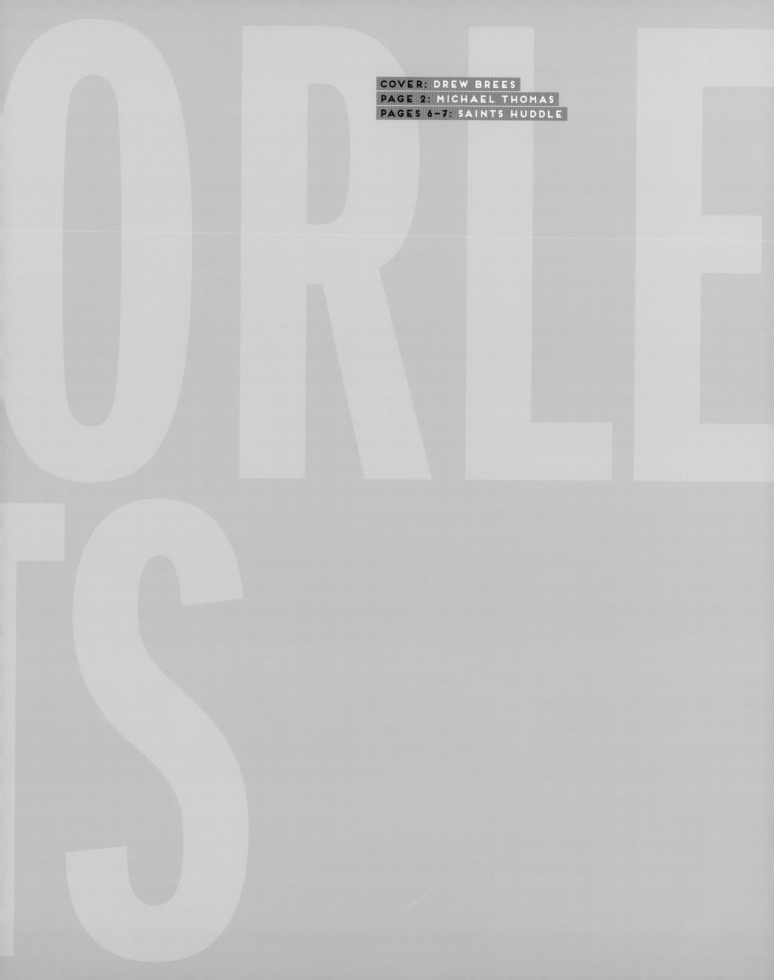

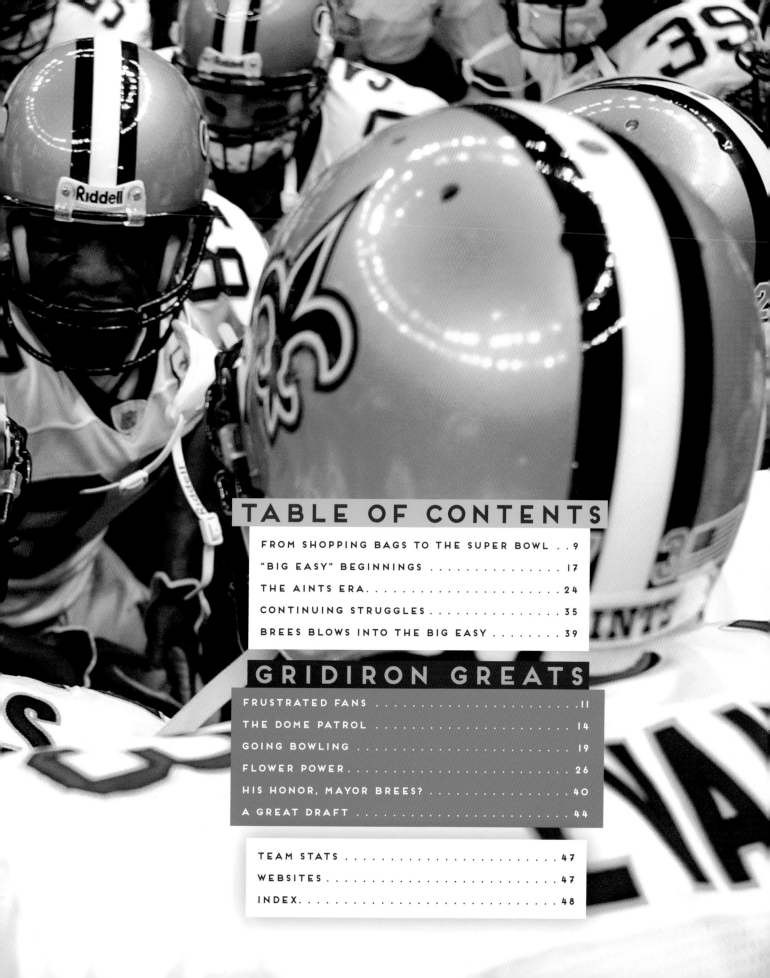

TABLE OF CONTENTS

GRIDIRON GREATS

FROM SHOPPING BAGS
TO THE SUPER BOWL

In the early 1980s, the New Orleans Saints was one of the worst teams in the National Football League (NFL). Ashamed fans wore paper bags over their heads because what they were seeing was so bad. They called the team the "Aints." But in 2009, the Saints reached the heights of the NFL. They were playing the Indianapolis Colts in Super Bowl XLIV.

There was no doubt that the Saints belonged in the big game. They had won the first 13 games of the regular season. Fans hoped for a perfect season. But the team decided to rest some of its starting players to keep them fresh for the playoffs. It lost the final three games of the season. But the Saints rebounded to crush the Arizona Cardinals in the first round of the playoffs. Then, they defeated the Minnesota Vikings in overtime. That earned them a spot in the Super Bowl.

The game took place in Miami's Dolphin Stadium. A few years earlier, Hurricane Katrina had caused massive destruction in New Orleans. The disaster was still fresh in the minds of people throughout the country. As a result, the Saints were the sentimental favorites to win. "Look around the stadium," said linebacker Scott Fujita. "It was like 6- or 7-to-1 [Saints fans]. The black and gold [the Saints' colors] just poured into Miami. The whole world was behind us."

There was one notable exception. Former Saints quarterback Archie Manning had been the face of the franchise during its early years. He still made his home in New Orleans. But his son Peyton was playing for Indianapolis. "I'm going to pull for my son," said Manning. "That's just the way it is. Anybody who thinks it's different must not have children."

The Colts bolted to a 10–0 lead. New Orleans responded with two second-quarter field goals. The Saints began the third quarter with a surprise onside kick. They recovered the ball. A few plays later, quarterback Drew Brees connected with running back Pierre Thomas for a go-ahead touchdown. The Colts came back. They gained a four-point lead. New Orleans kicked a field goal late in the third quarter. It cut the margin to a single point.

Late in the fourth quarter, Saints tight end Jeremy

LEFT: WIDE RECEIVER MARQUES COLSTON

GRIDIRON GREATS v
FRUSTRATED FANS

For many years, Saints fans were used to losing. But in 1980, even die-hard fans were embarrassed. One loyal fan, Bobby LeCompte, decided to hide his face. He found a paper bag. Then he cut holes for his ears, eyes, nose, and mouth. He placed a Saints sticker on it, and scrawled "Aints." The idea caught on. Soon, the Superdome was full of "Bagheads." The franchise tried to ban the bags. But fans kept wearing them. The Saints won just one game during the dismal season.

TRACY PORTER

"FOUR YEARS AGO, WHO EVER THOUGHT THIS WOULD BE HAPPENING WHEN 85 PERCENT OF THE CITY WAS UNDERWATER?"

—DREW BREES

Shockey hauled in a two-yard touchdown pass from Brees. A two-point conversion made the score 24–17. Less than six minutes remained. Colts quarterback Peyton Manning still had time to work his fourth-quarter magic. He led Indianapolis to the Saints' 31-yard line. He threw a short pass. Saints cornerback Tracy Porter jumped the route and picked off the ball. He raced 74 yards for a touchdown. The score put the game out of reach. The Saints were Super Bowl champions! One commentator called Porter's play "a perfect football moment."

Brees was the game's Most Valuable Player (MVP). "We just believed in ourselves, and we knew that we had an entire city and maybe an entire country behind us," he said. "Four years ago, who ever thought this would be happening when 85 percent of the city was underwater?... This is the culmination of that belief."

GRIDIRON GREATS ∨
THE DOME PATROL

The Saints made the playoffs for the first time in 1987. It was also the first year that linebackers Rickey Jackson, Sam Mills, Vaughan Johnson, and Pat Swilling played together. They were known as the "Dome Patrol." The NFL Network later called the foursome the greatest linebacker unit in league history. The Dome Patrol reached its peak in 1992. All four players were named to the Pro Bowl. It is the only time that has happened for four linebacker teammates. "Each was particularly good in one area, and it made the other guys better because as a unit they were so complete," said longtime Saints blogger Andrew Juge.

32

2

5

7

32 FUMBLES RECOVERED IN 1992

57 SACKS IN 1992

"BIG EASY" BEGINNINGS

New Orleans is nicknamed "The Big Easy." It is the birthplace of jazz music. The world-famous Mardi Gras festival takes place there, too. Its vibrant reputation was one reason the NFL awarded a franchise to the city in 1966. "N.O. Goes Pro!" shouted the headline of a local newspaper. A smaller headline advertised a team naming contest. But it was unnecessary. New Orleans is known for the jazz song, "When the Saints Go Marching In." "Saints" was the obvious choice. Businessman Dave

11

11 PRO BOWL SELECTIONS

189

189 GAMES PLAYED

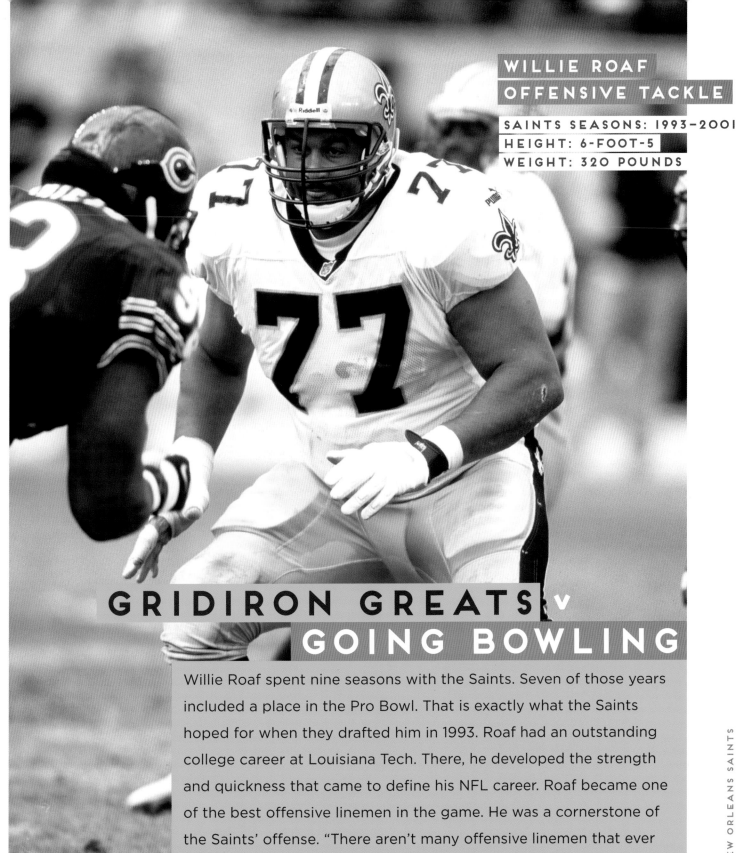

GRIDIRON GREATS v
GOING BOWLING

Willie Roaf spent nine seasons with the Saints. Seven of those years included a place in the Pro Bowl. That is exactly what the Saints hoped for when they drafted him in 1993. Roaf had an outstanding college career at Louisiana Tech. There, he developed the strength and quickness that came to define his NFL career. Roaf became one of the best offensive linemen in the game. He was a cornerstone of the Saints' offense. "There aren't many offensive linemen that ever played this game who had the athletic talent that he had and all the other things, too," said coach Jim Mora.

Dixon had overseen the team's admission into the NFL. He cleared the name with the city's archbishop. "I told him some gentlemen think somehow or another the name 'Saints' for our football team might be a little sacrilegious," said Dixon. The archbishop replied, "It's certainly not sacrilegious. Besides, I have a terrible instinct that we're going to need all the help we can get."

The archbishop may have seen the team's roster. It was comprised largely of aging castoffs from other teams and inexperienced rookies. At one end of the spectrum was 14-year veteran defensive end Doug Atkins. At the other end was rookie wide receiver Danny Abramowicz. The Saints lost their first seven games in 1967. They finished their first season with three wins. That set the tone for the next decade. They didn't even come close to a winning record.

Several players became stars. Abramowicz was among the league's top receivers in 1969. He had 73 catches. He piled up 1,015 yards and scored 7 touchdowns. In 1970, kicker Tom Dempsey made the record books. He was born without toes on his right foot. He wore a special square-toed shoe. He attempted an NFL record 63-yard field goal in the last seconds of a game against the Detroit Lions. The ball sailed through the uprights. The Saints won, 19–17. It was one of two wins that season. "They carried [coach] J. D. [Roberts] off the field like he was a hero," said sportswriter Peter Finney. "J. D. was on top of the world."

A new savior was on the way. The Saints chose Archie Manning with the second overall pick in the 1971 NFL Draft. He spent 10 full seasons in New Orleans. He set

TOM DEMPSEY

"WE'RE GOING TO BE THERE VERY SOON. THIS TOWN IS DYING FOR A WINNER, AND EVERYONE ON THIS TEAM IS DYING TO BE ONE."

—LINEBACKER JOE FEDERSPIEL

every team passing record. But even he couldn't guide the Saints to a winning record. In 1976, the team added speedy running backs Chuck Muncie and Tony Galbreath. Still, the Saints stayed at the bottom of the National Football Conference (NFC) West Division.

The Saints improved in 1978. They won seven games. Manning threw for 3,416 yards. He was named the NFC's Player of the Year. In 1979, Muncie became the first Saints player with more than 1,000 rushing yards in a season. The same year, young wide receiver Wes Chandler piled up 1,069 receiving yards. That was a team record, too. New Orleans finally broke even with an 8–8 record. "We're going to be there very soon," linebacker Joe Federspiel told reporters. "This town is dying for a winner, and everyone on this team is dying to be one."

CHUCK MUNCIE

THE AINTS ERA

DEFENSEMEN TONY ELLIOTT (NUMBER 99), FRANK WARREN (73), AND JIM WILKS (94)

The city's hopes were dashed in 1980. The Saints' defense collapsed. The team suffered its worst record yet: 1–15. Many games were not even close. Fans and newspapers began calling the team the "Aints." In 1981, the Saints featured running back George Rogers. He led the league in rushing with 1,674 yards. He was an easy choice for Offensive Rookie of the Year. Still, the team won just four games.

In 1982, the team traded Manning. "It broke my heart to leave the Saints," Manning said. "I think [new coach Bum Phillips] had a quick-fix agenda

GRIDIRON GREATS v
FLOWER POWER

A flower might seem an odd symbol for an NFL team. But the fleur-de-lis is no ordinary blossom. Its history extends back to the ancient Greeks. It is part of the logo for the Boy Scouts of America and the Chevrolet Corvette. After Hurricane Katrina, New Orleans residents drew the fleur-de-lis on walls. It was a symbol of hope and recovery. Saints players take pride in the unique logo. Defensive end Bobby McCray explained, "It's not like all the other logos in the NFL, like a simple animal or something like that. This is pretty distinguished."

and just wanted to win right away, with his guys." That year, the Saints won fewer than half of their games. They notched eight victories in 1983. But then they fell back to losing records.

Jim Mora took over as coach in 1986. During the hot Louisiana summer, he put the squad to the test. They ran post-practice sprints until they collapsed. "I was going to make an impression," he said later. Mora's approach lent New Orleans a new toughness. Rookie running back Rueben Mayes rushed for more than 1,300 yards. He was named Offensive Rookie of the Year. But the team still could not break even. The Saints finished the year 7–9.

The 1987 season started with a players' strike. One game was canceled. Teams used replacement players for several others. The regular roster returned on October 25. That day, the San Francisco 49ers topped the Saints 24–22. The loss inspired Mora's infamous "coulda, woulda, shoulda" speech. He talked about how his team

just was not good enough to win—yet. Linebacker Sam Mills said, "It made the guys think, 'Hey, we've gotta get the ball rolling.'" They did. The next Sunday, the Saints routed the Atlanta Falcons, 38–0. The victory launched a winning streak that lasted the rest of the season. The Saints finished 12–3. It was their first ever winning record. They marched into the postseason for the first time. But they lost to the Vikings, 44–10.

JIM MORA

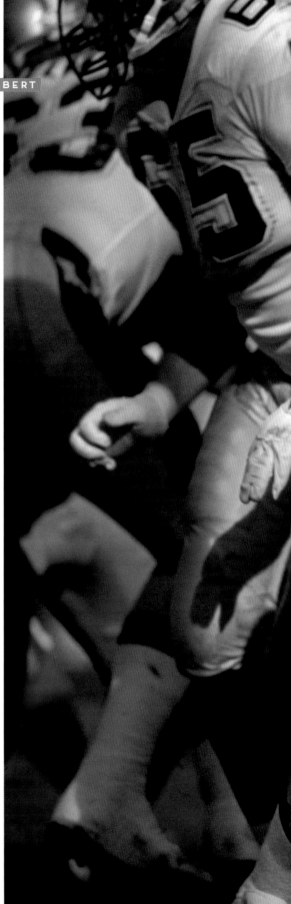

BOBBY HEBERT

The Saints made the playoffs again in 1990, 1991, and 1992. The defense featured a group of tough linebackers. Known as the "Dome Patrol," it shut down opponents. In addition, the Saints had finally found a replacement for Manning. Bobby Hebert proved to be a scrappy young quarterback. Despite the team's improvements, there was still another hurdle to overcome. The Saints had not yet won a playoff game. The Chicago Bears beat them in 1990. The Falcons came from behind in the 1991 playoffs. They beat the Saints, 27–20. The following season, the Philadelphia Eagles scored 26 points in the fourth quarter. They defeated the Saints, 36–20.

CONTINUING STRUGGLES

The Saints drafted Willie Roaf in 1993. He was a solid offensive tackle who went on to the Hall of Fame. But the team faded from the playoff picture with an 8–8 record. It posted 7–9 records for the next two years. The bottom fell out in 1996. New Orleans won just two games in the first half of the season. On October 20, they suffered a 19–7 loss to the Carolina Panthers. That was the last straw for Mora. He erupted in a post-game press conference. "It was an awful performance by our football team," he said. "We should be totally embarrassed, totally ashamed." Mora resigned that night. The Saints won only one more game that season.

The 1997 Saints strutted into the Superdome. They had a bold new coach. "Iron Mike" Ditka had coached the 1985 Bears to victory in Super Bowl XX. His hiring boosted season ticket sales. But Ditka could not lift the sagging Saints. The offense sputtered. New Orleans went 6–10 in 1997 and 1998. Ditka's solution was to trade eight draft picks to the Washington Redskins. In return, the Saints were able to select running back Ricky Williams in the 1999 NFL Draft. Williams had been a superstar in college. He won the Heisman Trophy in his final season. But he could not fix the Saints' offense by himself. The team stumbled through a 3–13 season.

Owner Tom Benson promised that things would change. "I will take whatever steps necessary to make the New Orleans Saints a winning franchise," he said. He started by firing Ditka. The Saints added quarterback Aaron Brooks. He connected with speedy receiver Joe Horn 94 times in 2000. It was a team record. The Saints surged to 10–6. They capped the season with a playoff victory over the defending Super Bowl champion St. Louis Rams. It was the first postseason triumph in Saints history. Brooks threw four touchdown passes. Special teams standout Brian Milne sealed the win. He pounced on a fumbled punt with less than two minutes left in the game. The Saints lost to the Vikings a week later. Still,

New Orleans had finally tasted postseason victory. It was hungry for more.

The Saints dropped to 7–9 in 2001. They traded Williams. In 2002, brawny running back Deuce McAllister ran for more than 100 yards in eight different games. But the Saints' struggles continued. They missed the playoffs that season and the next two as well.

DEUCE MCALLISTER

BREES BLOWS INTO
THE BIG EASY

In 2005, football became an afterthought in Louisiana. Hurricane Katrina devastated New Orleans and the Gulf Coast. Thousands of homes were destroyed. The Superdome became an emergency shelter. The Saints played their home games at other locations. They managed just three wins that season.

The team returned to the Superdome for a Monday Night Football game in September 2006. It was sparked by the energetic response of fans and the arm of its new quarterback, Drew Brees. The Saints won, 23–3. New Orleans finished the season 10–6. It topped the NFC South

HIS HONOR, MAYOR BREES?

The Saints faced a tough choice before the 2006 season. Should they take a chance on quarterback Drew Brees? He had played well with the San Diego Chargers. But he suffered a serious shoulder injury in 2005. After that, he became a free agent. The Saints signed him. It was one of the best decisions in team history. Brees is active in community affairs. He helped rebuild the city after Hurricane Katrina. He also donated money to the recovery effort. To the people of New Orleans, he is much more than a football player. "That grit Drew plays with, it's very much the personification of this city," said one Saints fan. "We have the mayoral elections. Brees could win as a write-in candidate. Brees is one of us."

DREW BREES
QUARTERBACK

SAINTS SEASONS: 2006–PRESENT
HEIGHT: 6 FEET
WEIGHT: 209 POUNDS

Division. It won a playoff game against the Eagles. But Chicago beat the Saints in the NFC Championship Game.

New Orleans fell short of the playoffs in 2007 and 2008. But in 2009, the Saints won 13 games. It was the best record in team history. They crushed the Cardinals in the playoffs. They faced Minnesota in the NFC championship. In the final 20 seconds, the Vikings were within range of the game-winning field goal. But Minnesota attempted a pass. Tracy Porter intercepted the ball. The game went into overtime. Kicker Garrett Hartley booted a 40-yard field goal. The Saints won, 31–28. That launched them to the Super Bowl. Two weeks later, they were Super Bowl champions.

New Orleans returned to the playoffs the following year. It was the heavy favorite against the Seattle Seahawks. Seattle had earned widespread ridicule for winning the NFC West with a 7–9 record. The Seahawks rode the momentum of a raucous home crowd. They knocked off the defending NFL champions, 41–36.

The next year, New Orleans won its last eight games of the year. It finished 13–3 for the second time in three years. The Saints topped Detroit in the playoffs. But they fell to San Francisco the following week. The thrilling matchup saw four lead changes in the final four minutes.

After going 7–9 in 2012, the Saints finished 11–5 in 2013. They returned to the playoffs where they edged out the Eagles, 26–24. But they lost to the Seahawks in the next round. The Saints reverted to 7–9 in the next three seasons. In 2017, they surged back to 11–5. They

DEFENSIVE END WILL SMITH

MARSHON LATTIMORE
CORNERBACK

SAINTS SEASONS: 2017–PRESENT
HEIGHT: 6 FEET
WEIGHT: 192 POUNDS

ALVIN KAMARA
RUNNING BACK

SAINTS SEASONS: 2017–PRESENT
HEIGHT: 5-FOOT-10
WEIGHT: 215 POUNDS

GRIDIRON GREATS v
A GREAT DRAFT

In 1967, the Associated Press began giving awards for Offensive and Defensive Rookies of the Year. That year, both rookies were Detroit Lions players. Fifty seasons later, the Saints became the second team to boast that distinction. Marshon Lattimore and Alvin Kamara (pictured) earned the honors in 2017. With five interceptions, Lattimore was an obvious choice. Kamara faced a challenge from Kansas City's Kareem Hunt. Hunt was the rushing leader that season. But Kamara was the second rookie in NFL history to have more than five rushing touchdowns, five receiving touchdowns, and a kickoff return for a touchdown. He also led the league with an average of 6.1 yards per carry.

5

5 INTERCEPTIONS IN 2017 (LATTIMORE)

728

728 RUSHING YARDS IN 2017 (KAMARA)

defeated the Panthers in the Wild Card. Then, they faced the Vikings. The Saints lost on the final play of the game. They returned to 13–3 in 2018 and marched into the playoffs. After beating the Eagles, the Saints faced the Rams in a close contest. Fans and players alike were upset by a controversial missed call late in the game. The Rams won, 26–23.

The once-lowly "Aints" have transformed themselves. Now, fans hope that their team will soon march to another Super Bowl championship. When that happens, historic New Orleans will echo with music and celebration once again.

NFL CHAMPIONSHIP

2009

NEW ORLEANS SAINTS

https://www.neworleanssaints.com/

NFL: NEW ORLEANS SAINTS TEAM PAGE

http://www.nfl.com/teams/neworleanssaints/profile?team=NO

NEW ORLEANS SAINTS

INDEX

TIGHT END
JIMMY GRAHAM